In Celebration of Our

*F*RIENDSHIP

KELLY WILLIAMS

A DayMaker Greeting Book

Thinking of you today...

No special occasion...

Just a celebration of our friendship.

Thank you for being my friend!

OLD
FRIENDS
ARE
TREASURES.

What Is a Treasure?

When you think of the word *treasure*,

you probably think of money...

maybe even jewels or precious metals.

But is a treasure something more—

something of far greater worth?

When I think of treasure, I think of you, my friend.

Over the years we have formed a relationship

that is more precious to me than any

material goods or riches the world has to offer.

Your friendship is more valuable than any rare gem

and more meaningful than

my most prized possession.

TREASURE YOUR RELATIONSHIPS, NOT YOUR POSSESSIONS.

ANTHONY J. D'ANGELO

As old wood is best to burn,
old horse to ride, old books to read. . .
so are old friends always most trusty to use.

LEONARD WRIGHT, *DISPLAY OF DUTIE*

The best mirror is an old friend.

GEORGE HERBERT

With clothes the new are best;
with friends the old are best.

CHINESE PROVERB

AH, HOW GOOD IT FEELS...
THE HAND OF AN OLD FRIEND.

MARY ENGELBREIT

The most I can do for my friend
is simply to be his friend.
I have no wealth to bestow on him.
If he knows that I am happy in loving him,
he will want no other reward.
Is not friendship divine in this?

HENRY DAVID THOREAU

For where your treasure is,
there will your heart be also.

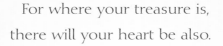

*My friends are
my estate.*

EMILY DICKINSON

I count myself in nothing else so happy
as in a soul rememb'ring my good friends.

WILLIAM SHAKESPEARE

I keep my friends
as misers do their treasure,
because, of all the things
granted us by wisdom,
none is greater or better than friendship.

PIETRO ARETINO

ONE WHO KNOWS HOW
TO SHOW AND TO ACCEPT KINDNESS
WILL BE A FRIEND BETTER
THAN ANY POSSESSION.

SOPHOCLES

Hold
a true friend
with both
your hands.

NIGERIAN PROVERB

Cherished Friend

GOD MUST HAVE KNOWN THERE WOULD BE TIMES

WE'D NEED A WORD OF CHEER

SOMEONE TO PRAISE A TRIUMPH

OR BRUSH AWAY A TEAR.

HE MUST HAVE KNOWN WE'D NEED TO SHARE

THE JOY OF "LITTLE THINGS"

IN ORDER TO APPRECIATE

THE HAPPINESS LIFE BRINGS.

I THINK HE KNEW OUR TROUBLED HEARTS

WOULD SOMETIMES THROB WITH PAIN

AT TRIALS AND MISFORTUNES

OR SOME GOALS WE CAN'T ATTAIN.

HE KNEW WE'D NEED THE COMFORT

OF AN UNDERSTANDING HEART

TO GIVE US STRENGTH AND COURAGE

TO MAKE A FRESH, NEW START.

HE KNEW WE'D NEED COMPANIONSHIP

UNSELFISH. . .LASTING. . .TRUE,

AND SO GOD ANSWERED THE HEART'S GREAT NEED

WITH A CHERISHED FRIEND. . .LIKE YOU.

AUTHOR UNKNOWN

NOTHING—
NOT EVEN TIME
OR DISTANCE—
CAN SEVER THE
BOND OF TRUE
FRIENDSHIP.

EVEN THOUGH WE MAY
BE SEPARATED BY MILES. . .
EVEN THOUGH WE MAY
GO FOR MONTHS
WITHOUT HAVING
A REAL CONVERSATION. . .
WE CAN ALWAYS PICK UP
RIGHT WHERE WE LEFT OFF.
THIS IS TRUE FRIENDSHIP.

Though our communication wanes at times of absence, I'm aware of a strength that emanates in the background.

CLAUDETTE RENNER

THE ROAD TO A FRIEND'S HOUSE IS NEVER LONG.

DANISH PROVERB

DON'T WALK IN FRONT OF ME,

I MAY NOT FOLLOW:

DON'T WALK BEHIND ME,

I MAY NOT LEAD:

WALK BESIDE ME,

AND JUST BE MY FRIEND.

ALBERT CAMUS

A friend is a hand
that is always holding yours,
no matter how close or far apart you may be.
A friend is someone who is always there
and will always, always care.
A friend is a feeling of forever in the heart.

COLLIN MCCARTY

A friend is someone
who knows the song in your heart
and can sing it back to you
when you have forgotten the words.

AUTHOR UNKNOWN

I Said a Prayer for You Today

I SAID A PRAYER FOR YOU TODAY,

AND KNOW GOD MUST HAVE HEARD.

I FELT THE ANSWER IN MY HEART

ALTHOUGH HE SPOKE NO WORD.

I DIDN'T ASK FOR WEALTH OR FAME,

I KNEW YOU WOULDN'T MIND.

I ASKED HIM TO SEND TREASURES OF A FAR

MORE LASTING KIND. I ASKED THAT HE'D BE NEAR YOU

AT THE START OF EACH NEW DAY, TO GRANT YOU HEALTH

AND BLESSINGS AND FRIENDS TO SHARE YOUR WAY.

I ASKED FOR HAPPINESS FOR YOU IN ALL THINGS

GREAT AND SMALL, BUT IT WAS FOR HIS LOVING CARE

I PRAYED THE MOST OF ALL.

AUTHOR UNKNOWN

Friends are always friends
no matter how far
you have to travel back in time.
If you have memories together,
there is always
a piece of your friendship
inside your heart.

KELLIE O'CONNOR

FRIENDS TOUCH
OUR LIVES IN
WAYS NO ONE
ELSE CAN. . . .
THEY LEAVE
LASTING IMPRINTS
ON OUR HEARTS.

OVER THE YEARS YOU HAVE MADE
A GREAT IMPACT ON MY LIFE.
THROUGH YOUR FRIENDSHIP
I HAVE GAINED MUCH DELIGHT.
YOU HAVE TAUGHT ME
TO LAUGH. . .TO RELAX. . .
TO CHERISH EVERY MOMENT
OF EVERY DAY. . .
TO ENJOY LIFE.
THANK YOU FOR GIVING ME
MUCH JOY AND HAPPINESS.
YOU WILL FOREVER
HAVE A PLACE IN MY HEART.

The best and
most beautiful things
in the world
cannot be seen or even touched.
They must be felt
with the heart.

HELEN KELLER

IT IS ONLY WITH THE HEART
THAT ONE CAN SEE RIGHTLY;
WHAT IS ESSENTIAL
IS INVISIBLE TO THE EYE.

ANTOINE DE SAINT-EXUPERY

Remember, the greatest gift
is not found in a store nor under a tree,
but in the hearts of true friends.

CINDY LEW

My friends are my heart, my soul,
my fun, my laughter, tears, love, and my life.

KATE TIERNEY

Our mouths were filled with laughter,
our tongues with songs of joy.

PSALM 126:2 NIV

*The greatest sweetener
of human life is friendship.*

JOSEPH ADDISON

A friend is one to whom one
may pour out all the contents of one's heart,
chaff and grain together,
knowing that the gentlest of hands
will take and sift it, keep what is worth keeping
and with a breath of kindness blow the rest away.

ARABIAN PROVERB

A FRIEND
IS SOMEONE
WHO REACHES
FOR YOUR HAND
BUT TOUCHES
YOUR HEART.

FROM *THE LITTLE PRINCE*

A FRIEND LOVETH AT ALL TIMES.

PROVERBS 17:17

Ointment and perfume rejoice the heart:
so doth the sweetness of a man's
friend by hearty counsel.

PROVERBS 27:9

Friendship is the inexpressible comfort
of feeling safe with a person,
having neither to weigh thoughts
nor measure words.

GEORGE ELIOT

DO NOT KEEP THE ALABASTER BOX

OF YOUR FRIENDSHIP SEALED UP. . . .

FILL [YOUR FRIENDS'] LIVES WITH SWEETNESS.

SPEAK APPROVING, CHEERING WORDS

WHILE THEIR EARS CAN HEAR THEM,

AND WHILE THEIR HEARTS

CAN BE THRILLED AND MADE HAPPIER.

THE KIND OF THINGS YOU MEAN TO SAY

WHEN THEY ARE GONE, SAY BEFORE THEY GO.

GEORGE W. CHILDS

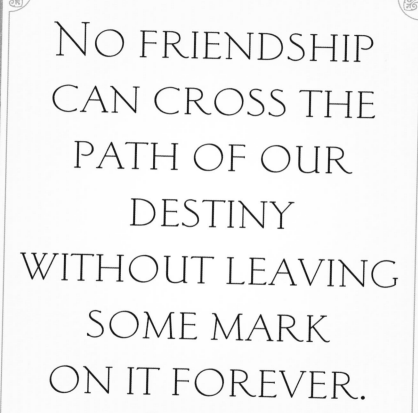

NO FRIENDSHIP
CAN CROSS THE
PATH OF OUR
DESTINY
WITHOUT LEAVING
SOME MARK
ON IT FOREVER.

FRANÇOIS MAURIAC

Life is full of people who will

make you laugh, cry, smile

until your face hurts,

and so happy that you think you'll burst.

But the ones who leave their

footprints on your soul

are the ones that keep your life going.

NATALIE BERNOT

FRIENDS SHARE
LAUGHTER,
TEARS, DREAMS,
DISAPPOINTMENTS. . .
AND EVERYTHING
IN BETWEEN.

ONE THING REMAINS A CONSTANT

IN OUR LIVES: AS FRIENDS,

WE SHARE MOST EVERYTHING—

FROM OUR EMOTIONS TO OUR WARDROBES,

NOTHING IS HELD BACK.

WE SHARE AN UNBREAKABLE TRUST.

THIS UNIQUE BOND ALLOWS US

TO BARE OUR SOULS TO ONE ANOTHER.

BECAUSE OF THIS—*BECAUSE OF YOU*—

I AM A BETTER PERSON.

WHEN WE HONESTLY ASK OURSELVES

WHICH PERSON IN OUR LIVES MEANS THE MOST TO US,

WE OFTEN FIND THAT IT IS THOSE WHO,

INSTEAD OF GIVING ADVICE, SOLUTIONS, ORCURES,

HAVE CHOSEN RATHER TO SHARE OUR PAIN

AND TOUCH OUR WOUNDS

WITH A WARM AND TENDER HAND.

THE FRIEND WHO CAN BE SILENT WITH US

IN A MOMENT OF DESPAIR OR CONFUSION,

WHO CAN STAY WITH US IN AN HOUR OF GRIEF

AND BEREAVEMENT,

WHO CAN TOLERATE NOT KNOWING,

NOT CURING, NOT HEALING, AND FACE WITH US

THE REALITY OF OUR POWERLESSNESS,

THAT IS A FRIEND WHO CARES.

HENRI NOUWEN

It is a curious thing in human experience
but to live through a period of stress and sorrow
with another person creates a bond
which nothing seems able to break.

ELEANOR ROOSEVELT

A true friend unbosoms freely,
advises justly, assists readily, adventures boldly,
takes all patiently, defends courageously,
and continues a friend unchangeably.

WILLIAM PENN

Friendship improves happiness and abates misery by doubling our joys and dividing our grief.

JOSEPH ADDISON

IF ONE FALLS DOWN,

HIS FRIEND CAN HELP HIM UP.

BUT PITY THE MAN WHO FALLS

AND HAS NO ONE TO HELP HIM UP!

ECCLESIASTES 4:10 NIV

The friend in my adversity I shall always cherish most.
I can better trust those who helped
to relieve the gloom of my dark hours
than those who are so ready to enjoy with me
the sunshine of my prosperity.

ULYSSES S. GRANT

FRIENDSHIP WITHOUT SELF-INTEREST

IS ONE OF THE RARE

AND BEAUTIFUL THINGS IN LIFE.

JAMES FRANCIS BYRNES

It is the character of very few men to honor
without envy a friend who has prospered.

AESCHYLUS

Anybody can sympathise
with the sufferings of a friend,
but it requires a very fine nature
to sympathise with a friend's success.

OSCAR WILDE

Friendship is a strong
and habitual inclination in two persons
to promote the good and happiness of one another.

EUSTACE BUDGELL

Friendship is essentially
a partnership.

ARISTOTLE

Friends. . .
They cherish one another's hopes.
They are kind to one another's dreams.

HENRY DAVID THOREAU

There are two things one should know
about the direction of his life.
First is: *Where am I going?*
Second is: *Who will go with me?*

ELIE WIESEL

*"Stay" is a charming word
in a friend's vocabulary.*

LOUISA MAY ALCOTT

Friends are as companions on a journey,
who ought to aid each other
to persevere in the road to a happier life.

PYTHAGORAS

*A friend is someone
who knows who you are,
understands where you have been,
accepts what you become,
and still gently
invites you to grow.*

WILLIAM SHAKESPEARE

I love you not only for what you are,
but for what I am when I am with you.
I love you not only for
what you have made of yourself,
but for what you are making of me.
I love you for the part of me
that you bring out.

ELIZABETH BARRETT BROWNING

God does notice us,
and He watches over us.
But it is usually through another person
that He meets our needs.

SPENCER W. KIMBALL

FOREVER FRIENDS. . .

Dear Lord, thank You for the gift
of friendship. Through this gift
You have given us love. . .comfort. . .
laughter. . .and countless blessings.
Help us to show our friends
how much they mean to us—
that they are indeed more valuable
than any riches of this world.
May we always look to You
for guidance as we hold these
delicate relationships
in our hearts and hands. Amen.

A friend is a person
with whom I may be sincere.
Before him I may think aloud.

A friend may well be reckoned
the masterpiece of nature.

Keep your friendships in repair.

The only reward of virtue is virtue;
the only way to have a friend is to be one.

I do not wish to treat friendships daintily,
but with the roughest courage.
When they are real,
they are not glass threads or frost-work,
but the solidest thing we know.

The glory of friendship
is not the outstretched hand,
nor the kindly smile,
nor the joy of companionship;
it is the spiritual inspiration
that comes to one when he discovers
that someone else believes in him
and is willing to trust him
with his friendship.

Life goes headlong.
We chase some flying scheme,
or we are hunted by some fear
or command behind us.
But if suddenly we encounter a friend,
we pause;
our heat and hurry look foolish enough.
A friend is the hope of the heart.

Never shall I forget the days I spent
with you. Continue to be my friend,
as you will always find me yours.

LUDWIG VAN BEETHOVEN

MAY THERE ALWAYS BE WORK
FOR YOUR HANDS TO DO.
MAY YOUR PURSE ALWAYS
HOLD A COIN OR TWO.
MAY THE SUN ALWAYS SHINE
ON YOUR WINDOWPANE.
MAY A RAINBOW BE CERTAIN
TO FOLLOW EACH RAIN.
MAY THE HAND OF A FRIEND
ALWAYS BE NEAR YOU,
MAY GOD FILL YOUR HEART
WITH GLADNESS TO CHEER YOU.

IRISH BLESSING

THANK YOU,
FRIEND,
FOR MAKING MY
WORLD BRIGHTER.
YOU HOLD A
SPECIAL PLACE
IN MY HEART—
NOW AND FOREVER.

DayMaker
GREETING BOOKS

© 2003 by Barbour Publishing, In

ISBN 1-58660-930-

Book design by Kevin Keller |designconcep

Photography credit: Cover and page 2, Calum Colvin; page 7, Jake Wyman; page 20, Lynn Jame
page 27, Ann Cutting; page 32, P. E. Reed; page 39, Kamil Vojnar (Photonic

Scripture quotations, unless otherwise noted, are taken from the King James Version of the Bibl

Published by Barbour Publishing, Inc., P.O. Box 71
Uhrichsville, Ohio 44683, www.barbourbooks.co

 Member of the
Evangelical Christia
Publishers Associat

Printed in Chin
5 4 3 2